Matter and Its Properties

by Mary Miller

PEARSON
Scott
Foresman

W9-BEJ-188

What are properties of matter?

Elements

An **element** is a basic building block of matter. There are more than one hundred different elements. Elements join together to make up all other kinds of matter. They cannot be broken down into smaller pieces.

Only a few elements are found in nature in their pure form. One element found in its pure form is gold. Most of the matter around us is made up of combined elements. For example, rust forms when iron combines with oxygen. Most living and nonliving things are made up of just a few elements. These elements are combined in many different ways.

This instrument smashes particles together, forming new types of matter.

You can identify an element by its chemical and physical properties. Chemical properties tell how one material changes into another material. Physical properties can be measured without changing the material. Physical properties include the color, smell, texture, or hardness of an object. Mass and volume are also physical properties. Each element has its own set of properties.

When you measure an object's physical properties, you do not change the object. When you observe an object's color, you have done nothing to change it. You can use rulers, microscopes, and thermometers to observe, describe, and measure physical properties. Scales and balances can also be used.

More than $\frac{3}{4}$ of elements are metals. The physical properties of metals include the following. Metals are shiny and smooth. They can be bent. Metals also conduct heat and electricity well.

Weight, Mass, and Volume

Weight is a measure of the pull of gravity on an object. Weight is measured by scales with springs in them. The more the springs move, the more the object weighs. Some objects are too big to fit on a scale. In these cases, each part of the object can be weighed, and the weights of all the parts can be added together.

Weight changes when the pull of gravity changes. Gravity is not the same everywhere on Earth. For example, the pull of gravity is weaker on the top of a high mountain than on level ground. Objects weigh less when they are farther from Earth's surface.

Mass is the amount of matter in an object. Mass and weight are not the same thing, although an object's mass affects its weight. If gravity gets weaker, an object's weight decreases. But its mass stays the same.

Mass is measured on a balance. Units of grams, milligrams, or kilograms are used. An object you wish to measure is placed on one side of the balance. Objects with known masses are placed on the other side until the two sides balance. In the photo below, the toy car is balanced by eight cubes that each have a mass of one gram. This tells us that the toy car's mass is eight grams.

Volume is the amount of space that an object takes up. Volume is measured in cubic units. To find the volume of a box, you measure its length, width, and height. Then you multiply the three measures together. You can write a formula that uses V for volume, L for length, W for width, and H for height. The formula for finding the volume of a box is $V = L \times W \times H$.

Since it takes eight grams of mass to balance the car, you know that the car's mass is eight grams.

A graduated cylinder can be used to find the volume of a liquid. It can also be used to find the volume of an object that can't be measured easily with a ruler. The object must be small enough to fit in the cylinder and sink in water. First, fill the cylinder about halfway with water. Measure the level of liquid. Place the object into the cylinder. Read the new volume of water. Subtract the volume of the water alone from the volume of the object and the water together. The difference between the two volumes is the volume of the object.

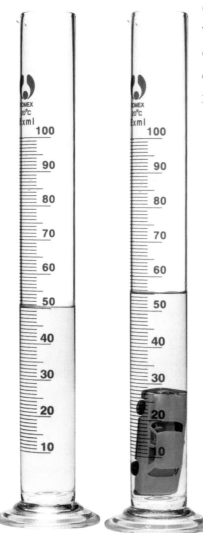

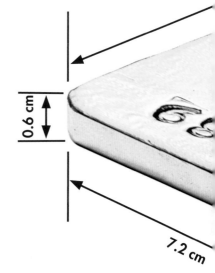

Properties of Objects and Materials

There is a difference between an object's properties and a material's properties. For example, one of the properties of a gold bar might be a rectangular shape. The bar has a certain size and mass. If you cut the bar, some of its physical properties as an object will change.

The properties of a material do not change. The gold bar can be bent, cut, or crushed, but the properties of gold stay the same. The shape of the gold does not change its density. If you cut it into little pieces, the pieces will still not be attracted to a magnet. Its color, hardness, and texture will not change either. These are properties of the material gold, not those of the gold bar.

2.3 cm

This gold bar has a mass of about 1,025 grams. You can find its volume by multiplying the length, width, and height.

Density and Buoyancy

Density is the amount of matter in a certain volume. Divide an object's mass (m) by its volume (V) to find its density (d). To find the density of a toy car with a mass of 8 grams and a volume of 5 cubic centimeters, divide 8 by 5. The density is 1.6 grams per cubic centimeter.

Density is a physical property. The density of a material does not change with the size of an object. For example, iron will always have a density of about 7.9 grams per cubic centimeter. The density will be the same for a huge piece of iron or a tiny piece. This property can be used to identify materials. Different materials often have different densities.

The ball of clay and the baseball both have the same volume, but the ball of clay has greater mass. This makes it more dense.

An object that floats is buoyant. Buoyancy is an important property in objects such as boats or balloons. It is very important that life jackets are buoyant to help people float on the water.

Buoyancy depends on the density of an object and the density of the liquid or gas around it. Fresh water has a density of about 1 gram per milliliter. Materials with lower densities than water, such as cork, will float in water. Materials with higher densities, such as iron, will sink.

Ocean water has dissolved salt and other minerals in it. These minerals make ocean water more dense than fresh water. The density of water depends on how much material is dissolved in it.

Mass and Volume

Even though iron is more dense than water, it can still be used to build a ship that floats. This is because a ship is not solid metal. It has lots of rooms and hallways. Most of its volume is filled with air. Because of all this air, the ship has much less mass than you would find in a solid piece of metal of the same size. This makes the ship's density less than water's density.

How do atoms combine?

Atoms

An **atom** is the smallest particle of an element that still has the element's properties. Atoms of one element are different from atoms of all other elements. The properties of atoms affect the properties of an element. The atoms' properties also control how the element can combine with other elements. Atoms are too small to be seen, even with a microscope.

The center of the atom is called the nucleus. The nucleus usually has both neutrons and protons. A **neutron** has no electrical charge. A **proton** has a positive charge. Atoms can be identified by how many protons they have. Only carbon atoms have six protons. If an atom has six protons, it must be a carbon atom.

Electrons move around the protons and neutrons. An **electron** has a negative charge. Electrons can join or leave atoms. They can also be shared by atoms.

Elements are organized in a table. It is called the periodic table of elements. Elements are put in rows based on their number of protons. Each of the table's columns contains elements with similar properties. For example, all elements in the last column on the right are called noble gases. All these elements are gases at room temperature, and they do not usually combine with other elements.

Every element has a symbol. It is made up of one, two, or three letters. Only the first letter of the symbol is capitalized. For example, the symbol for calcium is Ca.

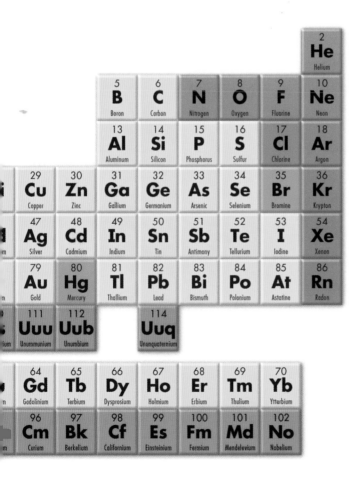

Compounds

A **compound** is a type of matter. It is a combination of elements. The atoms of these elements are joined together in a molecule.

The properties of a compound are different from the properties of the elements that make it up. Sugar is a compound. It has the properties of being a sweet, white solid. Sugar is made up of atoms of carbon, hydrogen, and oxygen. At room temperature, pure oxygen and hydrogen are invisible gases. Pure carbon atoms form black coal. On their own, these elements are nothing like sugar.

Sugar is a compound of carbon, hydrogen, and oxygen.

Molecules

Most substances are made of many elements. A molecule is the smallest particle of a substance that has the properties of that substance. The atoms of some molecules are bonded together by shared electrons. Some electrons no longer move around just one atom. These electrons can move around two or more atoms, bonding the atoms together.

Every molecule of a compound has the same elements and the same number of atoms. For example, every molecule of water has the same three atoms.

Every compound has a name and a formula. A formula is a sort of recipe for that compound. Water has the formula H_2O. The "2" after the "H" shows that there are two hydrogen atoms. The "O" stands for oxygen. There are no numbers after it. This means there is only one atom of oxygen in the molecule of water.

Salts

Some compounds are not formed by sharing electrons. The particles in salts are held together by opposite charges. These particles may be charged atoms or groups of atoms. Particles with more electrons than protons have a negative charge. Particles with fewer electrons than protons have a positive charge.

There are many types of salts. All of them have at least one metal element. Each salt also has one nonmetal element. All salts can form crystals. Crystals are created when charged particles form a geometric pattern. Salt crystals are brittle. Most salts will melt only at very high temperatures.

Table salt is sodium chloride. Its crystals looke like cubes.

Pure copper is a golden brown metal.

The properties of salts are different from the properties of the elements that make them up. For example, the table salt you sprinkle on food is made up of sodium and chlorine. On their own, sodium and chlorine can be dangerous. Pure sodium is a soft, silver-colored metal. Adding sodium to water can cause an explosion. Pure chlorine is a yellow, poisonous gas. But together, sodium and chlorine make a salt that is safe to eat.

Copper makes a green salt when combined with chlorine and water.

Copper makes a blue salt when combined with sulfur and oxygen.

How do phase changes occur?

Solids and Liquids

Water has three forms: solid, liquid, or gas. These three forms are called phases, or states, of matter. The phase of any material is due to the motions and arrangements of its particles. The phase that a material is in at room temperature is a physical property.

The particles in a solid are very close together. They vibrate, or shake, in place. The forces between the particles keep them from moving around. Solids have a shape and volume that does not change.

As a solid warms up, it can melt and become a liquid. The particles can now move and slide past each other. That is why liquids take the shape of any container they are placed in. Like solids, liquids have a volume that does not change. The particles might move but they remain close together.

When a liquid gets cold enough, it will freeze. Its particles will slow down and vibrate in place. A material freezes at the exact temperature that it melts. This temperature is called the freezing point or melting point. Water freezes when its temperature falls to 0ºC. Ice melts when its temperature rises above 0ºC.

Different materials have different freezing points. A material's freezing point is a physical property. It is always the same for that material. But if something is added to a liquid, its freezing point can change. For example, adding salt to water will lower its freezing point.

Materials change size when they change temperature. Material is not made or destroyed when this happens. The hotter a material gets, the faster its particles move. Faster moving particles have more space between them. This makes the material grow a little larger. When materials cool, their particles move more slowly. There is less space between the particles. So the material becomes a little smaller.

Material	Freezing or Melting Point
Oxygen	−218°C
Nitrogen	−210°C
Mercury	−39°C
Fresh Water	0°C
Sugar (Sucrose)	185°C
Lead	327°C
Aluminum	660°C
Gold	1063°C
Nickel	1453°C
Iron	1535°C

Gases

Particles in a gas are farther apart than particles in solids or liquids. The particles don't affect one another unless they bump together. A gas does not have a definite shape or volume. When a gas is put in a container, its particles spread out evenly throughout the container.

Evaporation takes place when particles leave a liquid and become a gas. This happens when particles at the surface of the liquid move upward quickly. If the temperature is high enough, particles in the rest of the liquid will also evaporate. As gas particles move up, they form bubbles. The temperature at which this happens is called the boiling point.

The boiling point is a physical property of a liquid. A liquid's boiling point will be the same no matter how much is being heated. Different liquids have different boiling points.

When water boils, liquid turns into gas at the surface and below the surface.

When clothes dry,
the water in them
evaporates.

A gas takes up more space than the liquid that evaporated to form it. This is not because there is more matter in the gas. It is because the particles of gas have more space between them than the particles of liquid.

Condensation is the opposite of evaporation. In condensation, a gas turns into a liquid. Condensation often happens when gas particles touch a cold surface. The particles slow down and become colder. They are trapped by the forces of the cold surface. As more gas particles are trapped, they form a drop of liquid. Dew on the grass forms by condensation.

What are mixtures and solutions?

Mixtures

In a mixture, different materials are put together. The materials do not bond as they do in compounds. The different materials keep their own properties. For example, salt and pepper can be mixed together. The salt and pepper do not change their color or flavor.

After being combined, the materials in a mixture can be separated. This is because they have different properties. If sand and iron filings are mixed, a magnet can pull out the iron. Iron has the property of being magnetic, but sand does not.

Separating a Mixture

A mixture of salt and pepper can be separated by using the different properties of the two materials. Salt dissolves in water. Pepper does not. Pepper floats on the water's surface.

1. The mixture of salt, pepper, and water is poured through a filter. The pepper cannot go through the filter paper.

While some metals are elements, many are mixtures of elements. For example, brass is a mixture of copper and zinc. These mixtures are called alloys. The properties of an alloy are different from the properties of the original metals in the mixture.

3. The water can be boiled away, leaving the salt in the dish.

2. The salt and water pass through the filter paper.

Solutions

If you mix dirt and water together, the dirt will slowly settle to the bottom. But if you add sugar to water, the sugar will dissolve completely. Sugar and water together make a solution.

A solution is a type of mixture. In a solution, the materials spread out evenly. Particles do not settle at the bottom. The substance that dissolves is called the solute. The substance in which the solute dissolves is the solvent. In a solution of sugar and water, the solute is sugar and the solvent is water. Water is called a universal solvent because it can be a solvent in many different solutions.

When a solute dissolves, its particles separate. These individual particles spread throughout the solvent. Solids dissolve faster when the liquid is heated or stirred.

A dilute solution has little solute compared to how much could dissolve.

A solution can be made from two liquids. A solution can also be a gas dissolved in a liquid. Water in a lake contains dissolved oxygen and carbon dioxide.

Solubility is how much of a substance can be dissolved by a solvent at a certain temperature. The hotter the solution, the more solute can be dissolved.

A **saturated** solution contains all the solute that a solvent will hold without changing the temperature. More solute can be added to a saturated solution, but it won't dissolve. A **concentrated** solution is one that is almost saturated. A **dilute** solution has a small amount of solute. Certain materials will not dissolve in certain liquids. For example, salt will not dissolve in oil.

A concentrated solution has a large amount of solute compared to the amount of solvent.

If you add more solute to a saturated solution, the extra solute will settle to the bottom.

Glossary

atom   the smallest particle of an element that has all the element's properties

compound   matter made up of a combination of elements held together by chemical bonds that cannot be separated by physical means

concentrated   having a large amount of solute in a solution compared to the amount of solvent

dilute   having little solute compared to how much could dissolve

electron   a negatively charged particle moving around the nucleus of an atom

element   a basic building block of matter that cannot be broken into simpler materials

neutron   a particle in the nucleus of an atom that has no electrical charge

proton   a particle in the nucleus of an atom that has a positive electrical charge

saturated   contains all the solute that can be dissolved without changing the temperature